The Authority of the Hadith

A Brief, General Reply to those who Refute or Undermine its Necessity & Integrity

by

Mufti Ahmed Yaar Khan Naeemi Ashrafi رحمة الله عليه

THE AUTHORITY OF THE HADITH

Translation of *Ek Islam* (One Islam) by
Hakīmul-Ummah Mufti Ahmed Yaar Khan ﷺ

Second Edition (2015).

Available as a free e-book.

Editor Maulana Omar Sayed

This book is free to be shared, printed and/or
distributed by any means, electronic or mechanical,
without consent from the publisher, on condition that
the text is not altered or obscured in any way.

Published by **Hedaaya Publications**
Greytown, South Africa

Learn more at **www.islamic-literature.com**

or e-mail us at **hedaaya.publications@gmail.com**

————————

Hadrat (حضرة) – Arabic prefix denoting honour; commonly
used by Muslims of the Indian subcontinent.

CONTENTS

ولا يحرمون ما حرم الله و رسوله

'(And the disbelievers) do not forbid what Allah ﷻ
and His Messenger ﷺ have made Haraam.'

– Surah Tauba (9), Verse 29

بسم الله الرحمن الرحيم

نحمده و نصلى على رسوله الكريم

INTRODUCTION

و ما ينطق عن الهوى ، إن هو إلا وحي يوحى

*"Nor does he speak by his own desire. It is no less
than revelation sent down to him."*
– Surah Najm (53), Verses 3-4

Undoubtedly, all utterances of the Holy Prophet 🕌 which are
part of the Deen are from Allah 🕌, The Wise. The content and
words He spoke by means of revelation (wahi) is known as *Quran*,
while the content which was from Allah 🕌 but whose wording
was the Holy Prophet's 🕌 is known as *Hadith*. This is why the
Quran is recited in Salaah while the Hadith isn't. There are three
categories of Hadith,

1. Hadith'e-Qawli – The utterances of the Holy Prophet 🕌.

2. Hadith'e-Fe'li – His daily actions.

3. Hadith'e-Sukūti – Someone doing something in his
    presence and he didn't prohibit it.

We now understand why the Quran is called *Wahi'e-Jali*
(Manifest Revelation) while the Hadith is called *Wahi'e-Khafi*
(Concealed Revelation). According to the Companions of the
Holy Prophet 🕌, the Quran and Hadith occupied the same level of
obedience because, after listening to the Holy Prophet's 🕌 Hadith
themselves, they didn't distribute his inheritance (میراث) even
though the Holy Quran commands so.

Because of our advent in this world at a later stage, we had to scrutinize and examine the many Ahadith. Those which undisputedly reached us as successive (متواتر) were regarded as acting upon the Holy Quran (e.g. the rakāts of Salaah, the rate of Zakāt, etc.) while those which didn't reach this level of indisputability were accepted according to the level of their narration.

In short, the Quran and Hadith are two necessary pivots of Islam, without which its shelter couldn't be supported. Today some people shut their eyes completely and reject the Hadith while still acting upon thousands of them. I will present the view of the Muslims in two chapters, the first of which will discuss the proofs of the necessity of Hadith, while the second will answer a few objections on the issue.

CHAPTER 1

PROOF OF THE NECESSITY OF HADITH

Quranic verses

يايها الذين ءامنوا أطيعوا الله و أطيعوا الرسول و أولى الأمر منكم

*"O you who believe, be obedient to Allah, the Messenger, and
those who have power of command amongst you."*
– Surah Nisā (4), Verse 59

Acting on the Quran is obedience to Allah ﷻ, acting on the
Hadith is obedience to the Messenger ﷺ, and the Jurists completed
obedience to the Sahaabah. If obedience to only the Quran was
necessary, why did this verse mention obedience to three?

و يعلمهم الكتب و الحكمة

*"Our Prophet teaches them the book
(i.e. the Quran) and wisdom."*
– Surah Baqarah (2), Verse 129

If there was no need of Hadith, why did this verse mention
wisdom along with the Quran?

و ما ءاتكم الرسول فخذوه ، و ما نهكم عنه فانتهوا

*"And take what the Messenger gives you; and whatever
he prohibits you from, stay away from it."*
– Surah Hashr (59), Verse 7

If accepting only the Quran was necessary, this verse would've
read, "And whatever We give you, take it; and Whatever We
prohibit you from, stay away from it." Thus, we deduce that
everything we receive from Rasoolullah ﷺ (be it the Quran or even
a single Hadith) must be taken completely.

من يطع الرسول فقد أطاع الله

"He who was obedient to the Messenger has obeyed Allah."
– Surah Nisā (4), Verse 80

If the Quran and Hadith are both regarded as revelation, acting upon the Hadith is obedience to Allah ﷻ.

و يحرم عليهم الخبئث

"The Holy Prophet prohibits impure things on them."
– Surah Āraaf (7), Verse 157

It's established from this verse that prohibition is also proven from the Ahadith. The prohibition of consuming the flesh of dogs and donkeys are both from it.

إنا نحن نزلنا الذكر و إنا له لحفظون

"Indeed We have revealed the Quran and
We alone are its protectors."
– Surah Hijr (15), Verse 9

We come to know that Allah ﷻ is the protector of the Holy Quran's words, meanings, commands, and all of its secrets. This is why its reciters (Qāris), Scholars (Ālims) and Mashaaikh will be forever found until the Day of Qiyaamat. The Hadith is a medium for the protection of these treasures. If this wasn't the case, the words of Salaah and Zakāt would be protected but not their commands and secrets. Bear in mind that Salaah and Zakāt can also mean *to dance* and *to wash clothes* respectively (amongst other meanings). In short, the greatest means of the Quran's protection is the Hadith.

Ahadith

1) The Holy Prophet ﷺ said, "I have been granted the Holy Quran and its likeness (the Hadith). Soon a person will be born who will say, "The Quran alone is sufficient for us." Beware! That which has been prohibited by the Messenger of Allah ﷺ is like that which has been declared Haraam by Allah ﷻ. Beware! Donkey meat is Haraam and every clawed animal (dogs, etc.) is Haraam." – *Mishkaat, Baabul-Itisaam with reference to Abu Dawud and Dārimi*

2) Rasoolullah ﷺ said, "I leave two things with you, and as long as you hold fast to them, you will not go astray. They are the Book of Allah ﷻ (the Quran) and the Sunnah of this Messenger (the Hadith). – *Mishkaat with reference to Muatta*

3) "He who remains separate from the congregation (of Muslims) has removed the rope of Islam from around his neck." – *Mishkaat with ref. to Ahmed and Abu Dawud*

4) "Wolves tear apart the sheep that leaves the flock. Shaitaan is the wolf ready to tear a Muslim apart. He who separates himself from the congregation will become his prey. Remain forever with the congregation." – *Mishkaat with ref. to Ahmed*

   Muslims have always accepted both the Quran and the Sunnah, so he who refutes the Sunnah has separated himself from the Muslim congregation and is exposed to the traps of Shaitaan.

5) The Holy Prophet ﷺ states, "He who eats from Halaal wealth, acts upon the Sunnah, and from whom people are safe from his cruelty is an inmate of Jannah." – *Mishkaat with ref. to Tirmidhi*

6) "My Ummah will be split into 73 sects. All are inmates of Jahannam except one." The Prophet ﷺ was asked concerning

which sect would not be the inmate of Jahannam and he replied, "The path upon which the Companions and I are on." – *Mishkaat*

7) "My Companions are like stars. Whoever you follow, you will attain salvation." – *Mishkaat, Baabu Manaaqibis-Sahaabah with ref. to Razeen*

Rational Proofs

1) The Hadith is what proves the Quran to be the Quran. We didn't see the Quran being revealed or Hadrat Jibraīl علﻴﻪ اﻟسﻼم bringing down revelation. The Prophet ﷺ told us that this is the Quran and we accepted it. This very utterance is Hadith. The refuters of Hadith cannot prove the Quran to be the words of Allah ﷻ without the Hadith.

2) It's the Hadith that establishes the Surahs, verses and contents of the Holy Quran. How else did we come to know of the amount of Surahs or verses revealed by Allah ﷻ? Refutors of Hadith could never establish these things.

3) Without the Hadith, we couldn't practice the Holy Quran. In several places, Allah ﷻ states, "Perform Salaah and give Zakāt." Refuters of Hadith cannot prove from the Holy Quran the method of Salaah & the amount of rakāts to perform or the amount of Zakāt & the manner of dispensing it. Likewise, all other commands of the Quran are comprehensively understood by the Hadith. It's as if the Hadith is the Quran's annotation.

4) Those who reject the necessity of the Hadith should eat dogs and donkey meat. Similarly, the Quran has classified only three or four animals as Haraam (e.g. swine, carrion, etc.). Prohibition of other animals comes and is established from the Hadith.

5) The relation between the Quran and Hadith, or the Sunnah and Farāid (compulsory acts) is similar to how water is necessary in the preparation of food. Without water, food cannot be prepared or eaten. Likewise, Quranic commands cannot be fulfilled or remain without the explanation of the Holy Prophet ﷺ. Salaah is compulsory, but folding the hands, reciting *Subhanallah...*, *At-Tahiyaat...*, Durood Ibrahimi and making Salaam are all Sunnah. The "People of the Quran"

should demonstrate a Salaah which is solely from the Quran and not assisted by the Hadith.

6) The Holy Quran can both grant salvation and lead astray,

يضل به كثيرا و يهدى به كثيرا

"Many are led astray by it and many attain guidance by it."
– Surah Baqarah (2), Verse 26

However, to remain with the truthful can only be a means of salvation,

و كونوا مع الصدقين

"Be with the truthful."
– Surah Tauba (9), Verse 119

اهدنا الصراط المستقيم ، صراط الذين أنعمت عليهم

"(O Allah) Guide us on the straight path, the path of those whom You have favoured."
– Surah Fatiha (1), Verses 6-7

Accepting Hadith and Fiqh (Islamic Jurisprudence) is the path of the Scholars, Saints and virtuous servants. Thus, this is the path of salvation. Refuting the Hadith is contrary to their path (and is therefore deviation).

7) The Quran is the Book of Allah ﷻ and the Holy Prophet ﷺ is the Noor of Allah ﷻ,

قد جاءكم من الله نور و كتب مبين

"Indeed Noor from Allah has come to you and a manifest book."
– Surah Māidah (5), Verse 15

Without light, a book offers no benefit. Likewise, without the utterances and explanation of the Holy Prophet ﷺ, the Holy Quran cannot offer benefit.

Also, bear in mind that only the Deen which possesses the Friends of Allah ﷻ is the true Deen, and that which doesn't is only falsehood. Only the branch which is connected to the roots bears fruits and flowers. The Saints are fruits from the tree of the *millat* (religion) of Islam. Before, hundreds of them emerged from the Bani Israel, but ever since their deen was annulled, sainthood ceased with it. Today there are many sects of Islam, but only the Ahle-Sunnah wal-Jamaat (Sunnis) have the Friends of Allah ﷻ. No deviant sect (including the People of the Quran) can present one. So Alhamdulillah, only the Ahle-Sunnah wal-Jamaat are on the path of truth.

14

CHAPTER 2

OBJECTIONS & ANSWERS

Objection 1 Allah ﷻ states,

و نزلنا عليك الكتب تبيانا لكل شيء

*"And We revealed to you the Book to clearly
expound everything."*
– Surah Nahl (16), Verse 89

**When the Holy Quran has explained everything, what need is
there for Hadith?**

Answer – The Quran is an expounded explanation of everything
for the Holy Prophet ﷺ, not for us fools. This is why Allah ﷻ says
'you' in the singular, not plural, since He's only addressing
Rasoolullah ﷺ. Can those who present this objection deduct the
rate of Zakāt from the Holy Quran?

Objection 2 Allah ﷻ states,

و لا رطب و لا يابس إلا فى كتب مبين

*"There's nothing wet or dry not mentioned in
the manifest book (i.e. the Holy Quran)."*
– Surah An'ām (6), Verse 59

**When everything is in the Holy Quran, what need is there to
take from the Hadith?**

Answer – Undoubtedly everything is in the Quran, but only the
perfect intellect can deduce its content. Pearls are found in the
ocean but only a diver can bring them up. Medicine is found in
pharmacies but only doctors can prescribe their usage.

Allah ﷻ states,

و لقد يسرنا القرآن للذكر

"We have made the Quran easy for remembering."
– Surah Qamar (54), Verse 22

When the Quran has everything and has been made easy, what need is there of the Hadith?

Answer – The Holy Quran has been made easy to memorize, not to deduce laws from. This is why the word 'للذكر' was used. No one ever became a hafiz of the Torah or Bible, whereas the Holy Quran is memorized by even children. This is what is meant by 'made easy'. If the Holy Quran was made easy for deducing laws, what need was there for the Holy Prophet ﷺ to teach it?

و يعلمهم الكتب و الحكمة

"And he teaches them the Book and wisdom."
– Surah Baqarah (2), Verse 129

Objection 4 The four Caliphs used to stop people from narrating Hadith. How then did the Hadith come about?

Answer – The Companions didn't stop the narrating of Hadith. Rather, they prohibited carelessness in narration so that no incorrect utterance was attributed to the Holy Prophet ﷺ. If they completely stopped the narrating of Hadith, the Deen would've perished because it cannot exist without it. Thousands of narrations of the Companions are found today. Once, Hadrat Abu Saeed Khudri ؓ narrated a Hadith to Hadrat Umar ؓ. He replied,

"Present a witness for this Hadith or I will punish you."

16

It was only until Ibn Ubai Kaab gave testimony to it that Hadrat Umar ⚬ accepted it. – *Muslim, Baabul-Istizaan*

It's established from this tradition that the Companions displayed great scrutiny in the narrating of Hadith so that Hypocrites wouldn't dare fabricate them. In the annotation of the above, Imam Nawawi ⚬ also cites the same reason for Hadrat Umar's ⚬ insisting of a witness.

The Holy Prophet ⚬ said to his Sahaabah,

> *"Narrate my Ahadith to people; and there's*
> *nothing wrong in doing so."*
> – Muslim, Vol. 2, Baabu Kitaabatil-Ilm

How then could the Caliphs have prohibited the narration of Hadith?

Objection 5 The Prophet ⚬ said,

> *"Besides the Holy Quran, don't transcribe anything from me."*

If Rasoolullah ⚬ prohibited the transcribing of Hadith, there should be no reason for the Hadith to exist. Only the Quran was permitted by him to be recorded, and so only the Quran is necessary to be followed.

Answer – There are a few replies to this,

1) It's surprising that you are refuters of Hadith yet you still use this Hadith as proof of your claim. How can you use the Hadith to refute the Hadith?

2) This narration was intended for people who memorize the Hadith. If they wrote it, the want to memorize the sayings of the Prophet ⚬ would've ceased.

17

3) Also, this Hadith was said when the revelation of the Holy Quran had commenced, and there was fear of the Quran and Hadith being mixed due to the transcribing of both. After some time (when people began to understand the difference between the two), permission to transcribe the Hadith was given.

Some narrations which show consent to transcribing the Ahadith follow,

1) At the time of Rasoolullah's ﷺ demise, he himself asked for paper and said, "Bring it to me so that I may write something for you not to be led astray." If transcribing the Hadith was prohibited, why did the Holy Prophet ﷺ intend doing this? Hadrat Abu Hurairah ؓ states,

> *"Amr ibn 'As ؓ used to write down*
> *Ahadith. I never did."*

2) On the occasion of *Hajjatul-Wada* (The Final Hajj), the Prophet ﷺ delivered a sermon. Abu Shah submitted, "O Rasoolullah ﷺ, write down these commands for me." The Prophet ﷺ replied, "Someone write it down for Abu Shah."

3) Hadrat Abu Bakr Siddique ؓ wrote down Ahadith pertaining to the rules of charity (صدقة) and sent them to his governors so that they could practice upon them.

4) People asked Hadrat Ali ؓ, "Which secrets of the Holy Prophet ﷺ do you have with you?" He replied, "Nothing except a journal which has a few Ahadith written in it."

5) Hadrat Umar ibn Abdul-Azīz ؓ wrote to Abu Bakr ibn Hazm,

"Search for the Ahadith of the Prophet 🌸 and write them down; for I fear the loss of knowledge."

Imam Bukhari 🕮 has dedicated an entire chapter on this in his *Sahih Bukhari* (called *Baabu Kitaabatil-Ilm*, i.e. Chapter on Recording Knowledge). All of the above-mentioned narrations may be found within.

Important note – It is truly surprising that the Holy Quran has stressed the transactions of loans to be written down for the sake of wealth not being ruined, while the Hadith is more important and exquisite than wealth. How then can there be a prohibition to note it down?

Objection 6 There are many inconsistencies in the Ahadith. One says that the Salaah at night is more excellent than the entire world, while another says that Jihad is more excellent than the entire world. One Hadith states that Rasoolullah 🌸 lifted both hands often in his Salaah while another states that he didn't. One Hadith stresses abstinence from the world while another teaches involvement in worldly affairs. From this, we ascertain that the Ahadith are fake, since the speech of the Prophet 🌸 cannot have inconsistencies.

Answer – You claim that there's inconsistency due to your lack of understanding, while there's no such thing here. In one regard, Tahajjud is more excellent, and in another, Jihad is. Initially the practice of the Prophet 🌸 was to lift the hands during Salaah, but he stopped it in time and this practice was annulled. Abstinence from the world in personal matters is good, and being informed in the ways of the world with regards to Deeni affairs which effect both Muslims and the Ummah is also good.

Why do you reject the Hadith due to being a person without practice? Merely reading translations of Hadith in Urdu or English doesn't suffice in comprehending this science. Familiarize yourself with this discipline and then see the blessings of the Prophet's ﷺ narrations. Have you read the Holy Quran? If you did, you would've raised this objection against it first.

The Holy Quran states that the world was created with the command of *kun* ("Be"), meaning immediately, but it says in another place that the world was created in a few days. At one juncture, the Holy Quran states that Allah ﷻ will not talk to disbelievers, yet in another verse, it says that He will. The Quran tells us to be kind to disbelievers, then it orders us to be harsh, severe and make Jihad against them. In one verse, the *iddat* of a woman is a year, while in another, it is 4 months, 10 days.

Will you now reject the Quran? Definitely not! So similarly, don't reject the Hadith. Just as how you would try to make sense of these seemingly conflicting verses, so too should you persevere in understanding the Hadith. There is no inconsistency in both. Your reasoning, however, is questionable.

Objection 7 Many Ahadith are illogical. One says that after setting, the sun presents itself in the Court of Allah ﷻ and makes sajdah. It then seeks permission and rises. However, geography teaches us that the sun doesn't disappear but keeps moving. When we have night here, America has day. Thus, accepting such narrations in this scientific age makes Islam an easy target for ridicule.

Answer – This objection is also due to a lack of understanding the Hadith. The Quran also contains verses which seem contrary to logic and intelligence. We are told in it that trees and plants make sajdah yet we only see them upright. So, however you wish to understand this sajdah for trees and plants, use it for the sun too. What the narration actually means is that the sun is in continuous obedience to its Lord and forever seeks permission to rise in the different parts of the world. This is understood by the actual Hadith and not from incorrect translations of it.

20

Objection 8 It is established from the Ahadith that the Four Caliphs gathered the journals of Hadith written by people and burnt them. If writing down Hadith was a good act, what need was there for this? Also, if the journals truly were burnt, how did the Hadith reach future generations?

Answer – Those journals which had the Quran and Hadith mixed within them and which people thought was the Quran entirely were burnt, such as the journal (or *saheefa*) of Hadrat Abdullah ibn Mas'ood ﷺ. Refer to *Bukhari, Baabu Jam'il-Quran* for documentation on this.

Another explanation is that those journals which contained both correct and incorrect narrations were destroyed. However, just as how the true Quran was saved after these journals were burnt, so too were the true Ahadith saved.

Refuters of Hadith! Apply your common sense! Just as how the Quran is required in our lives, so too is the Hadith and Fiqh (Jurisprudence) pivotal in the life of Muslims.

Objection 9 Ahadith have been written and compiled after the time of the Holy Prophet ﷺ and were not gathered in book-form during the prophetic era. Due to this, they have no credibility. Who knows whether they have been correctly written or not?

Answer – This very question can be raised against the Quran. During the time of the Noble Messenger ﷺ, the Holy Quran was not in book form. Rather, it was gathered during the time of Hadrat Abu Bakr Siddique ﷺ and only published in the time of Hadrat Uthman ﷺ. Vowel points (إعراب) were inserted after the Four Caliphs. Chapters, rukus, etc. were also emplaced a long period after. Who knows whether people wrote the Quran correctly or not?

Allah ﷻ blessed the Companions with exceptional memory, to the extent that some of them were huffāz of not just thousands, but hundreds of thousands of Ahadith. When the era of the Sahaabah was drawing to an end, books of the Ahadith were carefully compiled, and such caution was taken that the history and biography of every narrator was recorded. Like this, an entire science materialized (i.e. the Science of *Asmā'ur-Rijaal* or 'Biographies of Narrators').

Imam Abu Hanifa ﷺ, who was born in 80 AH, compiled *Masnanīdu Abi Hanifa*, and Imam Malik ﷺ, who was born in 90 AH, compiled *Muatta Imam Malik*. Imam Muhammad ﷺ compiled *Muatta Imam Muhammad*, etc. Imam Bukhari ﷺ was born in 194 AH, and what can be said about his compilation (i.e. *Sahih Bukhari*)! Before it, people used to memorize Ahadith just as how the Quran continues to be memorized. After the compiling of *Bukhari*, this tradition lessened.

Objection 10 Hadith is transmitted by only one person narrating from one individual, whereas the Quran states,

و أشهدوا ذوى عدل منكم

"And bring to witness two just people from amongst you."
– Surah Talāq (65), Verse 2

The narrations from single narrators are not credible in light of this verse, so those narrations whose narrator is only one Companion or one Tab'āi is definitely not worthy of acceptance.

Answer – There are two replies to this,

1) If this is your claim, then the Quran is also not safe, because one Jibraīl ﷺ brought the Quran to one Prophet ﷺ, who then transmitted it to his Ummah. So in light of this verse, the entire Quran is also not credible. According to you, there

should have been two prophets transmitting the Quran to the Sahaabah.

Today, on the information given by only one person, we ascertain the purity of water, the direction of the qiblah, food being Halaal, etc. If two witnesses were necessary at every juncture, the world would've been thrown into chaos.

And anyway, the Quran itself states that the testimony of a single person is credible,

و شهد شاهد من أهلها
"One family member of Zulaikha presented testimony."
– Surah Yusuf (12), Verse 26

We understand that the chastity of Hadrat Yusuf عليه السلام was proven through only one witness, and the Quran permitted this.

2) In the court of an Islamic Judge, a claim in financial affairs will be proven by the testimony of two witnesses; and in matters of adultery, four witnesses. In Deeni matters, the information given by only one person is credible. In the field of Hadith, the following rules apply,

* Successive (متواتر) Ahadith are necessary for definitive (قطعي) beliefs.

* In other laws (مسائل), famous (مشهور) Ahadith are necessary at places, and sometimes the narration of a single narrator suffices.

* However, only sound (صحيح) Ahadith are accepted in laws of Shariah.

* Even weak (ضعيف) Ahadith are accepted when it comes to proving excellence (فضائل).

All of these rules are comprehensively discussed in *Usūl* (Principles of Islamic Jurisprudence). Shouldn't they be understood by you before deeming the Hadith to be a false science?

Objection 11 The content of some Ahadith disrupts Imaan. One Hadith states that the Holy Prophet ﷺ held the hand of the foreign woman Amīma bint Joon and wanted her interest turned towards him. However, she sought his protection from this. – *Bukhari, Kitaabut-Talāq*

Laa Hawla wa Laa Quwwata! If this is the content of Ahadith, how can they be accepted?

Answer – You didn't learn the Hadith from a distinguished teacher, and for this, you failed to understand its correct meaning. Recite 'Laa Hawla...' on your intelligence. Without understanding, this objection can be raised against the Quran as well.

The Holy Quran mentions the incident of Hadrat Lūt الـعلـيه. To save the honour of his guests, he said to his nation,

هؤلاء بناتى إن كنتم فاعلين
"These are my daughters if you wish to do so."
– Surah Hijr (15), Verse 71

Regarding Hadrat Yusuf الـعلـيه, the Holy Quran states,

و لقد همت به ، و هم بها لو لا أن رءا برهن ربه
"Zulaikha intended Yusuf and Yusuf intended Zulaikha."
– Surah Yusuf (12), Verse 24

Tell me, is Imaan not disrupted by presenting your daughters to the nation or intending foreign women? Do such things befit the

24

glory of prophets? Alhamdulillah, the Prophets عليهم السلام are free from defects.

The woman mentioned in the objection (Amīma bint Joon) was a woman who had entered into the nikāh of the Holy Prophet ﷺ. She was not a foreign woman. This is explained even in *Bukhari Sharif*. By his "daughters", Hadrat Lūt عليه السلام meant the wives of the men of the nation (i.e. the daughters of the nation). The complete translation of Surah Yusuf's verse is, "Zulaikha intended Yusuf and Yusuf too would've intended her if he didn't see the proof of his Lord." May Allah ﷻ grant true understanding of His words and comprehension of the narrations of Rasoolullah ﷺ.

Objection 12 It's a historical fact that the compilers of Hadith (محدثین) had thousands of Ahadith but they themselves regarded most of them as wrong and chose not to narrate them. From hundreds of thousands, Imam Bukhari رحمه الله kept only a few thousand in his book. From this, we come to know that incorrect narrations have been fabricated.

Answer – Yes, narrations were fabricated, but after the strife of the compilers, these fabrications were sifted out. Your objection in fact proves that they removed questionable narrations. Some didn't even record them in their books, while those who did pointed out their classification. *Tirmidhi Sharif* is an example of this. With every Hadith, Imam Tirmidhi رحمه الله wrote down whether it was sound, weak, etc.

Important Note – In conclusion, I wish to explain two things,

THE DIFFERENCE BETWEEN HADITH & SUNNAH

Hadith is the Holy Prophet's ﷺ every utterance or action which has been narrated, irrespective of whether it's practical for us to follow or not.

25

Sunnah is the Prophet's ﷺ every utterance or action which is practical for us to practice upon. Rasoolullah ﷺ keeping 9 wives at one time in nikāh, making tawāf of the Kaaba while riding a camel, or carrying his granddaughter Sayyidah Amaamah ؓ on his shoulder while performing Salaah are all proven from the Hadith but they are not regarded as Sunnah because we cannot practice upon them. This is why the Prophet ﷺ said,

عليكم بسنتي

"Hold onto my Sunnah."

He didn't say, "Hold onto my Hadith." So, no one can be *Ahle-Hadith* ("The People of Hadith") in the world. Through the grace of Allah ﷻ, we are Ahle-Sunnah because it means practicing upon the Sunnah, and this *is* possible. The same is not true for Hadith.

WHY ARE WE THE AHLE-SUNNAH?

Although we complete Fardh, Waajib, Mustahab and Nafl acts, we are not considered Ahle-Fardh, Ahle-Wājib, etc. because Fardh and Wājib etc. are only related to us after we reach maturity and are *āqil* (able to differentiate). On the other hand, the Sunnah is linked to us as soon as we are born. Making nikāh is Sunnah, eating and drinking is Sunnah, doing business is Sunnah, earning livelihood is Sunnah…in fact, even living and passing away is Sunnah. Fardh is only to cover the *satr* from the navel to the knee. All other things are Sunnah.

May Allah ﷻ grant us the ability to live and die on the Sunnah of His Beloved ﷺ. Ameen.

www.ingramcontent.com/pod-product-compliance
Lightning Source LLC
Chambersburg PA
CBHW030012040426
42337CB00012BA/754